"As someone who indulge~~s~~
it's reassuring to know ther
there. Scott Cumming is on
However, you will be able t~~o~~ .... within
this chapbook, whether you know who Steve Brule is
or not. There is something for everyone, and you will
enjoy the many layers. I would recommend sitting
down with a tasty beverage, this chapbook, some
mellow songs playing in the background, and dive in
headfirst."
  — **Andrew Davie**, author of *Dig Two Graves* and
  Ouroboros

"In this new chapbook, Scott Cumming offers a
collection of deeply expressive, confessional poems
that glide between lightheartedness and
heartbrokenness. Even the humorous poems are
stitched with melancholy threads, like a man telling a
joke while thumbing a razor blade. It's a delightful
collection, scuffed and rough-edged with dark
poignancy."
  — **C.W. Blackwell**, Author of *River Street
  Rhapsody*

"Bold, deep, funny, irreverent, Cumming delights
with this debut collection taking the reader through
the peregrinations of a father and husband fighting
his daily anxieties with humour, honesty and sharp,
beautiful lines."
  — **B F Jones**, author of *Artifice* and *Five Years*

"What's the deal with Scott Cumming? I'll tell ya what the deal is. Scott Cumming is the cool kid at the lunch table you wanna sit with. Scott Cumming is the dude at the bar who says 'wanna see something?' then proceeds to do a backflip without spilling his beer. Scott Cumming is the Marvel superhero we all want. The one who can save us from all the bad guys forcing us to read boring poetry. A Chapbook About Nothing is full of heart and humor and sincerity. It's an achievement that should come with its own national holiday. Read it and weep, peeps."

— **Shawn Berman**, Author of *Mr. Funnyman* and Editor of *The Daily Drunk*

FIRST CUT

A Chapbook About Nothing

by
Scott Cumming

Close To The Bone Publishing

Close To The Bone
Rugby
Warwickshire
United Kingdom
CV21

www.close2thebone.co.uk

Interior Design by Craig Douglas
Cover by Scott Cumming

First Printing, 2021

Contents

◆

About the Author

Scott Cumming unsuspectingly went to see Garden State wearing his Shins tee. He still contributed to the Kickstarter for Zach Braff's next film. He has been published at *The Daily Drunk, Punk Noir Magazine, Versification*, and *Shotgun Honey*. His poem, *Blood on Snow*, was voted the best of Outcast Press Poetry Things We Carry issue and nominated for a Pushcart.

He lives in Scotland with his fiancé and two sons and has never had a pet.

Twitter: @tummidge

Website: scottcummingwriter.wordpress.com

For
Vicky, Bruce & Cole
Kyle
Steve

A Chapbook About Nothing

Skyline

The skyline shows us what we want to see.
A destination.
An aspiration.
Our expiration.

City lights blot out our nightly wonders.
The roosting scatters the morning dim.

The skyline shows us what we want to see.
Forced isolation.
Growing alienation.
Damned desperation.

Sunset blinding us through the trees.
A squash of blue pushing against the gloom.

The skyline shows us what we want to see.
My resignation.
Loss of sensation.
Prescription medication.

Playing

I wonder
what her body looks like
underneath that parka
but it's not me
thinking this
Bukowski illusion
playing at being great
trying to stay warm
pacing back and forth
muttering his poems
beneath my mask
pandemic protection
or hiding ordinary madness
hands and fingers numb
letting you have your fun
escaping our hex
for an hour or so
even as air
floods our bones with cold
you and I
just little boys
each playing
at being real.

Birthday Surprise

We were eight when we found out
Caesar was murdered on your birthday.
A running joke
Throughout our friendship.
Even as we grew up
Tangled together
Complicated.
Memes, GIFs, Movies
Kenneth Williams to Brando.

Roman politics replaced
With everyday shite.
Drinking
Fighting
Fucking my wife.
All over a
A petty slight.
Time to cut you
From my life.
Closest thing I have:
This battered old bread knife.

Violence in Real Life

The superhero and the drunk
Stagger and sway
Our group stopped
In the middle of the road
Deciding where to go

Unintelligible yells
Signal something coming
The drunk swings
The superhero drops
Head hitting kerb
Like my head wants a pillow

The bouncer unmoved
Unwilling
Allows the drunk back inside
Decision made
Onward we go
No witnesses to a possible killing.

Steve Brule Face

It's hard not to disrupt the home schooling
With thoughts on John C. Reilly and Liam Neeson
It's hard not to pull a Steve Brule face
Pondering the 15 years of action and comedy
I'm willing to bet that on the set
Of The Gangs of New York
They placed a bet on
Who could upend their career in the wildest way
Perennial Oscar bait cast aside
For Euro directors and Adam McKay
They keep on in search of a winner
A non-stop cold pursuit into carnage
Guess we'll know it's over
When they crop up together
In a gross display of PTA.

D.C./Dad

DRUGS HAUL FOUND ON BOAT
"There's Dad's baldy head"
WIFE BRUTALLY MURDERED BY HUSBAND
"He looks like a Teletubby with that on"

The fun of seeing our father
Onscreen outweighed the tragedies
Of numerous crimes scenes

Not in wildest dreams
Could I envision the things
He's seen

While I play in this sandpit
Depicting horrors,
I can barely imagine
A testament to your fatherhood
That we never saw the headlines,
We only saw you.

To be Written Upon Waking

You wake to the winter dark
Closing in immediately
Targeting the heart

The slow, stabbing pain
Informs
It is one of those days

Where the mask will
Be required
Just to make it through

Pain squeezes
Your stomach
Pronouncing unworthiness

Reading doesn't soothe
Eyes spinning at the words
Leeching away all meaning

Feeling fraudulent
Already spent
Before the day's even begun

Writing this down
As a way not to drown
And destroy the days of four.

Playlist

Your playlist
is Feeling Happy
But I want Feeling Beat Up
Feeling spat out
Feeling depressed as hell
but I will never tell.

Safety in Members

My space and place in time
require me not to think
My skin, my dick
Totems of freedom
from living with fear.

I've approached too fast
then hung back
don't know which was worst.

I can cavort and cajole
with no alleged misdirection
no perceived intention.

I've blanched at the voice
inside my head
but I've never had to consider
the possibility of ending up dead.

In getting from A to B
no worries about option C.

Popping to the shop, scared
when it should be as simple
to breathe.

No longer allowed
to mourn or grieve
Lesser evils so much easier
to intervene.

Drips

The molasses drips
Mingles with the blood
She screams again
Maybe grief
Maybe pain

The cum drips on the sheets
Another two weeks, and blood again
She screams once more
This time frustration
This time menstruation

We try and we try
She bleeds and she bleeds
She screams and she screams
For those unborn
And never to be

We drift and we drift
Business-like breeding
Now I wish she'd scream
In pain, elation or
Even in hate

The sweat drips down our foreheads
It looks like there is too much blood
One final scream and a push
Every moment seems worth it
To see those eyes and that smile
Again.

Hi Angry. I'm Dad.

Everyday rage. It's nothing big that will cause an explosion. It's the incessant demands, orders, bickering, needling, taunting, not listening that will lead to something shouted you can't take back. The only thing that accepts STOP is the bloody wi-fi speaker!

Fire requires fuel and you are oversaturated with it on a daily basis. Bombs in miniature, detonating ever quicker.

A continued war for one, pushing your borders further and further out while the walls of your house creep closer and closer. Are you alienated or alienating? Are you trying to chill out or hide out? Is everybody the same?

Peering

Throwing a ball to yourself
As you wait for your child in the sub zero
Frigid cold dark, peering
To see if the night is as black as your heart
Wondering: does this shit even work?

The sanitiser on dried, cracked knuckles
Helps the pain seep deeper
Cleansing and sore like this medicine
My dark clouds and I float separately
Ready to tussle over bullshit once more.

A Walk to Clear My Head

I stare at the broken hourglass
Time's long been shattered
Couldn't tell you if I've missed
Or added a day of pills

One more post-rock album choice
Busting out my special moves
For an afternoon
Of fetishising on the edge of an abyss

Another overweight white guy
Cradling his useless ennui
Looking forward to the movie adaptation
With the mega star walking aimlessly
Dick in hand
£17.99 to rent.

No Name #6

feel depressed as fuck today
no reason why
can't summon the will
to do the things I love

staring at the void
within me
pushing it out
in long, loud sighs

talking helps
hard to find the words
when we all feel the same
with nobody to blame
nothing to point to

writing it down
to try and purge it
this time
another crumpled ball
thrown at the internet.

Small Talk Balk

For years we've sat mere feet apart
Yet I'll never share what's in my heart

I've got all these things I could say
One liners that would fucking slay

I read all the time
But I will never recite for you a single line

In darkness I dwell
Though you'll only ever know that things are well

My apathy shapes and strangles me
Evaporates the light others want to see

Memes, GIFs and comments
Won't make up for my monosyllabics

In all the time we've shared
I've barely a minute to spare.

The Lost Art of Air Guitar

Do people still play air guitar?
Rock 'n' Roll is dead
But do we still feel the need
To air shred?

Low single figures
The number of mirrors
I've encountered
And not felt the need
For a pout
And fake power chord

The adoring crowd of one
The perfect guitar strap and plectrum combo
The microphone stand sitting just right
Ready for non-stop anthems
In the greatest show of all time

Then your partner walks in
And you wouldn't feel as embarrassed
If it was the other thing
That would be more understandable
Than playing at being another cocksure demi-god.

The Home Office as Every Concert and Club Night That Should've Been

Hitting delete on that out of office e-mail
while listening to dance music from the noughties
as though you're dropping the best effect
is the new air guitar

Enter your password to unlock
as if you're nailing the keyboard solo
always need that green icon
acting as an alibi

Hurt your wrist on the desk
doing air drum fills
Scream into your water bottle
microphone
Pretend those prescription drugs
are something more

Argue nonsensically with your belligerent children
mimicking your favourite scuffles
Order a drink from the waitress
and practice chat up lines
even though she's your wife

And for that extra touch of
authenticity
You can always "end" the night
by dropping your phone in the toilet
with the wife's hairdryer
set up as hand dryer
to wave the battery port under.

Will everybody be fine if I elope with my Halloween episode Wanda FUNKO POP?

We can build our own Westview
And have superpowered FUNKO kids
Without hassle or scrutiny
celebrating Halloween in the 90s each day

It'll last as long as Jimmy Woo and crew
allow. A love bound by your hex
If you can love a butler turned synthozoid,
why can't I love you?

Those lacking vision will never understand
what those pink leggings do to a man
let us embrace in a dark hold
shut them out
and we'll make the best Home Improvement parody
possible

I follow the red lace
like wool strung upon a conspiracy map
my gaze lingering, persevering
before taking off in a quicksilver dash
lest I become just another enchanted Bohner.

My Dad will understand less of this than he did my Wanda poem

I'm so out of touch with the zeitgeist
I don't know if Rick and Morty is cool
Or if it was
And we're in the midst of the backlash phase

I called my 6-year-old Squanchy today
It's fine
since he's halfway to the age
where I might burst in
Then turn around
apologising for my rudeness

I always laugh at Rick burping out words
But as soon as a child tries it
I am demanding pardons and excusals
Farts are different
They're always funny
From anybody

Jerry is the successor to Homer J.
A man dumb enough to laugh at
A man real enough to uncomfortably push breath from my
mouth knowing I've done
something just like his latest calamity
And how I was completely fine about it
Until Jerry did it.

Losing my Edge on the School Run (Daft Dad is taking you for a playdate at my house)

Yeah, I'm losing my edge
I'm losing my edge
The kids are staring me dead in the eye
I'm losing my edge
I'm losing my edge to parents from Germany and from China
But I was there

I was there in 1979
I was there when Siouxsie and the Banshees split up
I said, don't end it this way.
I'm losing my edge
I'm losing my edge to neighbours whose banging
I hear when I'm singing in the shower
I'm losing my edge to the internet theorists who can
Tell me every plotline to every good comic from
1958 to 1997.
I'm losing my edge.

To all the parents on Instagram and Twitter
I'm losing my edge to the film noir cinephiles
In little jackets with more time to rewatch
Michael Mann movies than I do.

But I'm losing my edge
I'm losing my edge, but I was there
I was there
But I was there

I'm losing my edge
I'm losing my edge
I can hear the banging every morning in the shower.
But I was there
I was there at the first Sons and Daughters gig in
Aberdeen
"How do you know the words?"
Because I bought the album, obviously
I was there in 2003 when The Flaming Lips replaced
The White Stripes at T (Jack White – forever unforgiven)
Closest to religion I've been
With psychedelic Jesus leading me heavenward
I was there
I was the first guy on dancefloor at Exodus
I even cleared one once
Everybody thought I was crazy
I was there
I was there
I've never been wrong

I did work experience in a record store
I had everything on release day
I was there in the Estaminet DJ booth with
Chris Knox.
I was there at The Tunnels when Le Reno Amps
Covered Cash.
I woke up naked in somebody else's tent at a festival
In 2003.

But I'm losing my edge to better parents with
Better temperaments and more up-to-date references
And they're actually really, really nice

I'm losing my edge

I heard you have a playlist of every good cat video
Ever done by everybody
I heard you can recite every good quote from The Office
Every great quote by Michael Scott
All the minor characters
All the Creed Bratton quotes
I heard you have access to every
Major streaming platform
I heard you're working on a ranking
Of every Seinfeld episode
I heard that you have DVDs of every great 60s heist flick
And another shelf from the 70s

I hear you're buying a projector and a big screen
And are throwing your computer out the window
Because you want to watch them as they're intended
You want to feel like an auteur

I hear that you and your clique have sold your mountain
bikes
And bought Pelotons
I hear that you and your clique have sold your Pelotons
And bought road bikes

I hear everybody that you know has more followers than
everybody that I know

But have you seen the music download files that I bop to
instead of speaking to you?
Hot Hot Heat, always take a sweet in my pocket for the
boy,
The Mars Volta, Primal Scream,
The cool leggings with the see thru thigh bit,
The Bravery, Duke Special, Clap Your Hands Say Yeah,
Male pattern baldness, The Dead 60s,
Nine Black Alps, Longview, the top down Porsche,
The Eighties Matchbox B-Line Disaster,
Pink Grease, Be Your Own Pet,
The midnight showing of the first Transformers movie,
It was the new E.T.

Glasvegas, JJ72, Wolfmother, Mumm-Ra, We Are
Scientists, Art Brut, CSS.

Roots Manuva, Secret Machines, My Latest Novel,
Soulwax the band,
The childminder everybody has used, but us,
David Ford,
ELEC! TRIC! SCOOTER!
The Rakes, Feist, Menswear, Half Man Half Biscuit,
Zwan, The Electric Soft Parade, The Horrors,
The Sonic the Hedgehog bags,
The Sonic the Hedgehog bags,
The Sonic the Hedgehog bags,
The Sonic the Hedgehog bags,
The Sonic the Hedgehog bags,
Now stop-pah!

LCD are Sitting Next to Us at the After Party

LCD are sitting next to us at the after-party
How many furtive glances and admiring stares before we
say hi?

Coming across all nonchalant while fangirl fainting inside
It's the bassist's birthday and he just wants to get high

Happy birthday, sorry you can't get off your head
Enjoy this vodka and coke instead

We were the muso stoner indie kids
Not the ones sniffing coke off toilet lids

His situation normally all fucked up
Aberdeen not a patch on that NY scene

Too easy to forget how special these nights were
Just hope you find many more wherever you are.

April's Fool

Your funeral is set
for noon
on April Fool's Day
I'd be totally fine
If all the pain was in vain
A misjudged deep fake
You sprang up and out
And just walked away.

Live Stream

The final nail in my grief
Is seeing the coffin
On the video relay screen

Imagining your body
Dressed up
Nowhere to go
Ready to rest

No chance of chatting
About glory days
No epiphanies
No changing ways

Just crusted remnants of tears
And memories of dance floors
Concert halls
Summer festivals
You taking the piss
Because we went to see Hope of the States
Instead of Pixies

No chance to wistfully
Daydream about the new batch
We'll never see
No last dance
To The Rapture and LCD
Memories that'll never be.

I Understood the Assignment, I just didn't do it

Seems everybody knew
When they were teens
Reading King and Harris

I, on the other hand
Too embarrassed
To admit to not

The school book report
I fangled together
The night before it was due

Only read to page fifty
A sex scene that turned
Into an ambush

Completed and handed in
Thought nothing of it
Until I was ambushed
By the English Head

Seemed less trouble
To be painted
As a teenage deviant
Than admit to not reading.

Middle Class Tough

We were middle class tough
My friends and I
Wielding our penknives and scars
Attempting to perfect the
Knife trick from Aliens

The less adept
Practicing with sticks
In the dirt
Never quite gutsy enough
To do it properly

I didn't get in trouble
That time I stole out-of-date
Beer from our shed

Probably did my Dad a favour
Flatter than the tyres of the abandoned car
We drank it on

Flatter than the national team performance
That saw us humped and pumped
To an inevitable first round exit.

Teen Turf War

The school playing fields
An artillery barrage on traffic
During snowy weather
Getting chased, caught and
Fake names of accomplices a must

"Dare ye to get this car!"
In my ignorance I do
Sparking a near teen turf war
I'm tripped, kicked, drifted
For not giving a shit

Flashing blue lights signal
A mammoth rapid retreat
To gullies and meadows
Frozen boggy trenches and
High slippery branches
Fuck knows who the cop is chasing

This was the night I learned
You never return to the scene of the crime.

The Skywalks

The memory comes flooding in
Like a cheap bottle of cider
Guzzled down greedily

The woodland behind our neighbourhood
The skywalks, a mass of tangled
Branches, strong enough to hold
Hordes of children

The scorched earth and smashed bottles
Allow for tall tales of
Biker gangs and the supernatural

The first sight of a lady's nethers
Spied in a discarded magazine
In a long-abandoned house

The dangerous ones with
Scrambler bikes
Can't scare us down from our perches

With darkness
Comes the added danger
Of a deathly drop
But somehow none of us ever got hurt.

Imagining Bob Dylan auditioning for a TV talent show if he'd been born 40 years later

1.
Next, we have Bob
who has recently recovered from
a devastating motorcycle crash

Hi, I'm Bob and this is an original composition...

...The answer, my friend-

Sorry, Bob, I'm going to cut you off there
I'm not really sure we can sell this
Do you dance or anything on top of this?

*Uh, no, but I have some other songs
If you don't like that one.*

Okay, let's hear another then.

...Not that way, I wasn't born to lose-

Sorry, I need to stop you again
Undertakers, organ grinders
It's really not working for me
Anything else?
Something brighter, perhaps?

...About having to be scrounging your next
MMEEEEE-HAAAAALLLLLLLL-

Bob, Bob, Bob!
That was a better song,
But the singing just isn't working for me.

I can sing a little different too, if you
Can give me one more chance?

Sure, sure
One more time then.

...Lay across my big brass bed-

Bob *waving arms*
Bob
I don't think we can sing that type of song
these days.
I'm afraid it's a no from me.
Guys?
Sorry, Bob, four no's.
Good luck in the future.

2.

We have a familiar face for the judges
as he returns with pal Johnny
to try and compete in the groups section.

I'm Bob Dylan...
...And I'm Johnny Cash
And together we are
Jobby Dash.

Interesting name, guys.
I recognise you from a few weeks ago, Bob
I'll keep an open mind.

...a true love of mine-

Thanks, guys.
A very beautiful song,
But Johnny, your voice
overpowers Bob's way too much.
Bob, you sound better than before,
but I don't think I can sell you.
Johnny, I think you should audition
In a solo capacity.
Bob, sorry, but no from me again.
Three no's and a yes this time.
Good luck, guys.

3.
Johnny attended a solo audition
He made it to the finals
But was knocked out in week 3
When the youthful audience
did not take to his rendition
of an old gospel song

Bob boosted the subscriber figure
on YouTube from 26
to a few thousand
and in an effort to make a meagre dime
switched on the ad revenue function
on the site
only for an original subscriber
from the North of England
who commented
solely
"Judas"

Did The Avengers really think things through before carrying out The Blip?

On highways, one ways and runways
People appearing in the same place
as 5 years before
Into thin air, into sea
Climber undusting upon a mountain
that's eroded microscopically
Missing his foothold
plummeting soundlessly

Babies returning screaming in fright
Their parents moved on
Divorced
Could no longer stand the sight
of each other
and the empty crib

Spouses rematerializing in the marital bed
Replaced, removed,
now reduced to third wheel
witnessing the upgrade
mad in their stead

Sporting events and concerts
disrupted too
One moment to the next
That fly ball is gone
No axe left to grind

Imagine all building work
was suspended
for 5 years
It'll still suck for the people
in that helicopter though

Am I wrong to assume
that populations
across the universe returned
to possibly compromised
situations?

How many returned
only to face a new
more horrifying death?
How many families
quaked in hope,
only to grieve again?

Did the Avengers really think this through?

Evened the odds
when they resurrected Gods
but with all your genius IQs
Did you stop to think if you should?

Or did you take the necessary precautions
Ensure complete victory as we all assume?

I cheer and I cry
when the Portals open
Now I'll be thinking of
all those poor fuckers
falling from the sky.

Knuckleball Sandwich

Not all home runs are created equal
Tatis, bat flips, Bartolo
The one thing that unites us
Constantly excites us
The rush of blood
The rush to the mound
Helmets thrown
Gloves off
Blows traded
Like low level prospects
Benches clear
With vows of showing
What a real knuckleball
Looks like
Televised bar brawls
With sixty guys
Jostling and sparring
For supremacy

More repercussions
Or unwritten rules
Than I'll ever know
Tuning in The Show
For the promise of something
More than sport
More than the romanticism
Of high summer
The allure of pettiness
And grudges
You see in any workplace
Exploding with a bean
Or in the only place

Throwing behind someone
is the ultimate form
of disrespect.

Used

Nobody wants to be squandered
At the edge of existence
Money and attention
Enough to make you want to say yes
To whatever they want

Essential shoppers
Round at all hours
Dealing in plain sight
No nurses, no check ins,
No help

Getting used for a tiny amount
Still feels better than being left
To rot on the periphery
Friends until it ends
The police knocking in your door

So many questions you don't understand
Just mates, you tell them
Playing computer games, lending a hand
No, they tell you
Washing you away
Left to take the blame.

All of Which

In amongst
the hood rats
loose gats
prison tats
back to a life
on the wrong side
of the cracks
gotta get paid
any way you can
laid off
cut loose
your American dream
vamoosed
swirling the gutter
diving back down
at first sight
of crumpled dollar signs
doped up smiles
for watered down vials
wrong avenue
wrong time of day
roaming any territory
no guts, no glory
no gang ink
just a white boy
scrabbling
to put dinner
on the plates
unlikely
to end great
we all know
which pandemic

Goin' to end first
only question is
you goin' ta
take the time
ta read the rules?

Hurts

Newly broken heart
Fresh black eye
You should see
the other guy.

Broken ribs
Telling fibs
He hurt the kids this time
and you can't lose them.

Faceful of scratches
A backful of lashes
Sex games gone deranged
There are no safe words
In the depths of Strangeways.

Another icepack
Another swollen cheek
Beaten out
Of lunch money again
Next time you'll be carrying
More than a few quid.

Nose spread across his face
Defend the jab again and again
No ground game, shoot the leg
Successful takedown
Choke him out, leaking blood
Down his back.

The world turned crimson
Can't feel your legs
Or remember the last thirty seconds
The booze still spinning
The woman pïnned
Head bent the wrong way
Cannot run from the end
Of another godawful day.

The End is Here

A little house
You on the floor
The ultraviolence
Turned to gore

A slanted bone
Under the porch
Red wine boxes
Set aflame by torch

Blood rituals
in April snow
Crucifixes
For chopping wood

All my friends
Are Avatars
Slice of light
That never shines

Honest politics
Are now a myth
Read my lips
Paid sponsorship

Likeable characters
From social teams
Diversity
Shouldn't need to be screamed

Fingers poke
Out from the loam
Another mystery
Turning cold

Storage container
Shipped to icy shores
The banging, screaming
Paid to ignore.

Questioning

Curiosity killed the rat
Asking after
What they've
Never cared for before

Snitches don't get stitches
But unmarked watery graves
With no teeth
no fingertips
no prayers.

A Universal Truth

It is a universal
and unspoken truth
that most of us
have slept in
cum
at one time
or another.

The Unbearable Being of Lightness

The first cut is always the weakest
I return to slice and probe
Get close to the bone
Elicit truths
Between the tendons and veins

Nothing there
but more of the same
Questions asked from comfort

Kundera was right
Though I mostly remember
the dog

Never had a pet
And when we do
Naming duties lie elsewhere
Otherwise I might name one
After him.

I look in the mirror

How many times a day
do I scrape the hair
from my eyes?
How many times a day
do I fall in love?

When did I last
scrub my face?
When did I last
douse it in petrol
and set it aflame?

You Can Slide Anytime

I feel unworthy
Of my own pain
"Talk anytime"
Tiny face and name

I sit in the dark
Staring down walls
There is no balm
Only myself to blame

"DM, if you need to"
Requires a courage
My cowardice has never had.

Fixer Upper

Wrapped in a warm embrace
House insulated with those you love
Their bodies lining the walls

Bloody artworks
Decorate rooms
Finger-mark etchings
Of crude runes

Making a house
a home
Hard work to the bone
to the tendons
the nerve-endings

Sound-proofed,
Like any good neighbour would
Against agonised screams,
Beseechments,
prayers unanswered
Before quiet acceptance
Placidity
Resignation

Cupboard under the stairs
Secreting a corner
damp with tears
Mould forming
A layer of
lost regrets.

Overtakes Me

It overtakes me
Daily
This sense of dread
A fear of not being
Good enough
strong enough

It overtakes me
Suddenly
The emotional toil of
Looking back at mistakes
Guiltily
Helplessly

It overtakes me
Suffocating
My eyes and face
Locked on their final moments
It wasn't enough to create
No catharsis
No cure
Cannot imagine the depth
of their pain
Doesn't soothe
me though

It overtakes me
Blinding
To the happy way
I felt yesterday
This feeling
no victory can erase

It overtakes me
Shakes me
Decorates me
in a mascara of tears
Too scared to talk.

Running Until We Run Out

We float through the desert
On our way to becoming
Another set of American cliches

Did those before us
Find what they wanted here
or did they simply run out
Of land on which to flee?

Snow tyres don't drive so well
On sand dusted roads
Don't lick red snow
be wary of ice holes

The guilt swells
Like his eyes
Tyre ironed out
No longer a pretty sight

The dozen of them
With wagons rounded
Force us to kiss
Batter us for our sins

Opportunity presents
Gifts for avenging "fairies"
A hunting party man lost
Cut down staring at those
He finds gross

This truck was once a symbol
Of all our tenderness and truth
But that's rusting away
In pools of oily blood

The only clouds out here
made of our vapour
the reassurances we utter
Nothing more than hot air

We drift into another Red State
Is it illusory to think
Things will be better here?
Can you really run from hate?

Power Murder Ballad

The birds scatter on gunshot wings
slapping and snapping at the branches
as I fire up the circular saw

The pulsing sting
of mutual betrayal
beats in only one of us now

I remember when we had nothing, but
allergy medicine spiked into each of our legs
licking the drip of epinephrine blood from your thigh
falling deeply into the pool of our shared shallow breath
shaking with ecstasy as we elicit final sighs

As I ponder
this daylight decapitation
staring as appendages I once gripped
ravenous for every piece of you

Knowing I am poorer for your death
not just because you never told me
where the money is
But upon realising the wealth of my dearth

I killed our love
with a bathroom fuck
chasing the precipice, I reached
between your legs

Now I've killed you too
with heavy heart and deadened soul
I cut through your bones
hearing only our blissful moans

The night descends
The crows shooting back to their perches
My limbs wracked with regret
Wrapping up every piece of you.

The Daily Battle

I have no enemies
Except myself
there are no lofty expectations
but my own

Still, the thoughts linger
A constant buzzing drone

Lacking any perspective
Imposter in my own home
Masquerader in my comfort zone

A detriment to my health
this warring with myself

And yet,
Each poem is a balm
A therapy session to
Inflict no harm.

Acknowledgements

He will be wonderfully modest and shrug it off, but
without Stephen J. Golds, I wouldn't have read a poem,
let alone written a book full of them.

Max Thrax has been my confident confidant, an
inspiration and a constant support through my writing
journey and I wish to thank him for his time and
wisdom.

Vicky, Bruce and Cole deserve medals of some sort for
putting up with a demented, daft and embarrassing Dad
of the highest order. May nowhere be safe from our
antics.

Thanks, Dad, for reading everything even when you
don't understand it. Thanks, Mum, for always keeping
me right and telling me off for childhood transgressions
revealed decades later.

Thanks to Shona and David for your support. Knoxy and
Phil for your feedback and always being the first to be
sent many and various of my links.

Thanks to the many tiny names and avatars, that I
believe are linked to real, living beings, who have shown
me support with my writing (I feel Oscar speech likely
to have forgotten someone here) - B.F. Jones, Andrew
Davie, Shawn Berman, James Lilley, David Cranmer,
John Bowie, Paul D. Brazill, Justin Bryant, William R.
Soldan, J.B. Stevens, Curtis Ippolito, HLR, Fred Shrum
III, Mark Pelletier, J. Travis Grundon, Matthew Gomez,

M.E. Proctor, N.B. Turner, Kirstyn Petras, Amy-Jean Muller, J. Archer Avary and Anthony Neil Smith.

Grateful to the following places for previously publishing poems within:

The Daily Drunk
Punk Noir Magazine
Fevers of the Mind
Versification Zine
The Five-Two
Skyway Journal
Yellow Mama
Alien Buddha Press

Printed in Poland
by Amazon Fulfillment
Poland Sp. z o.o., Wrocław

86035574R00045